GLEN STANCIL

The Art of Discernment

Mastering the Practice of Wise Decision-Making

**HARG
BOOKS**

First edition

ISBN (paperback): 978-1-967982-01-1
ISBN (hardcover): 978-1-967982-02-8

This book was professionally typeset on Reedsy.
Find out more at reedsy.com

To Kerry - Thank you for the decades of helping me make great decisions.

To Bethany - Thank you for acting as a second conscience and sharing your knowledge with me.

To Alan - Thank you for living a life of service to others and demonstrating the legacy one can leave when one makes wise decisions.

To Matilda, Laurie, Eli, and Tracy - Thank you all for teaching me more about myself and sharing your expertise and mentorship.

"Discernment is not knowing the difference between right and wrong. It is knowing the difference between right and almost right."

C. H. Spurgeon

Contents

Introduction

Why Discernment Matters

In a world of infinite choices, fast-paced decisions and overwhelming information, the ability to wisely discern has never been more important. Discernment is not just about choices; it is the act of selection that aligns with our core values, goals and truths. It is a skill that touches every area of life from relationships to careers, finances, and spirituality in our daily lives.

Ask yourself this question: How many times have you questioned a choice you made? Perhaps you found a job that looked great on paper but left you feeling unfulfilled in your life, the result that is now being reflected by a lack of motivation. Or perhaps you did trust someone who shouldn't have had your best interests at heart. These moments, however difficult, illuminate a crucial truth: discernment is not perfection, but intention, clarity, and learning.

Discernment is not a skill limited to monks in monasteries or philosophers living in ivory towers; it's a practice, a toolkit that we can all use in our lives every day. But many of us were never taught how to practice it. We are living on autopilot, pulled in divergent directions by emotions, social expectations and the clamor of the contemporary world. The result? Decisions made in haste, regret of missed opportunities, and the sense of disconnection from ourselves.

This book is how to change the story. It is a map for recovering the power of discernment, for slowing down, turning inward and acting like your true self. It helps you find the clarity you need. Whether you are facing a decision that will change your life or just managing your daily "to-do list", this book's principles will provide clarity as well as a balanced and confident perspective for you.

What Is Discernment?

Discernment, at its deepest level, is the capacity to accurately judge. It's not only about knowing what's right and wrong, but also about knowing what is best and appropriate, what's more relevant, or what fits best for you personally. It's the superpower that enables you to cut through the internal noise and the nugget of truth that is right for you.

Discernment is not a one-size-fits-all process. It's intimate and demands personal introspection, thoughtfulness and practice. It's asking the right questions:

- Is this decision in accordance with my own values?
- What is the path that intuitively indicates to me?
- Am I acting out of fear, stress or genuine desire?

This book answers these questions and many more for others who need it.

Why Discernment Matters Now More Than Ever

Life as we know it today is fast and relentless. As we navigate confusing and sometimes contradictory messages from various sources: social media, news, and advertising, we are bombarded with conflicting information about who we are supposed to be and what we should want. Decisions, large and small, become progressively complicated.

But the pressure to deliver them perfectly and quickly can be paralyzing. By not discerning, we can become reactive rather than intentional. We may follow paths dictated by others rather than forging our own. Sometimes we might say "yes" when in fact "no" is more appropriate, embracing the comfort zone rather than being courageous and confident.

Imagine an existence in which you feel that every decision is meaning-filled and you really trust your gut, to feel comfortable in the face of the unknown. Picture a life away from regrets, living rooted in your values and goals.

This is the life discernment makes possible.

What This Book Offers

In *The Art of Discernment: Mastering the Practice of Wise Decision-Making*, you learn practical strategies for developing and strengthening your discernment skills. This isn't purely theoretical, it can be done. In this book, you will explore:

- How to align your decisions with your values and long-term goals.
- Ways to quiet mental and emotional clutter so you can see clearly.
- Tools to recognize and resist external pressures that steer you away from your true path.
- How to seek wise counsel and trust your intuition without losing objectivity.

Each chapter is written to help guide you step-by-step using reflection exercises and insights to deepen your understanding of the benefits to be gained by applying discernment into your daily practice.

A Personal Invitation

As the author, I come to you not as a perfect practitioner of discernment but as someone who has wrestled with its challenges and reaped its rewards. My own journey has been filled with choices, with some wise ones and others less so. But through it all, I've discovered that discernment is a practice, one that grows stronger with intention and effort.

This book is an invitation to join me on this journey. Together, we'll explore what it means to live a life guided by wisdom, clarity, and purpose. Discernment isn't a destination; it's a lifelong practice. And as you cultivate this skill, you'll find that the rewards extend far beyond making better decisions and transform how you experience life.

1

The Foundations of Discernment

What Is Discernment, Really?

Discernment is often misunderstood as knowing the difference between right and wrong. While that is partially true, discernment is far more nuanced. It's about being able to see the shades of gray within a situation, to see what is best to do in a particular moment, and to act aligned with your values and vision when you act and not from blind faith in a scheme of events. Rather, it's finding the clarity that lets you slice through all that noise of competing information, emotional turmoil and external pressure to make the best decisions for you that are in your best interest.

Think of discernment as a guide. It doesn't tell you where to go, but it helps you find your way. It doesn't guarantee you'll never take a wrong turn, but it ensures you're navigating with purpose and intention. The beauty of discernment is that it's not about being perfect, it's about being mindful, reflective, and wise.

Why Discernment Is a Skill, Not Just an Instinct

Many people believe that discernment is something you're either born with or not. This couldn't be further from the truth. While some individuals may naturally be more reflective or intuitive, discernment is a skill that can be developed and refined through practice.

At its heart, discernment requires three key components:

- **Self-awareness:** Understanding your values, beliefs, and biases.
- **Clarity:** The ability to quiet distractions and focus on what truly matters.
- **Reflection:** Taking the time to evaluate options, consequences, and alignment with your goals.

These components work together to help you see beyond surface-level appearances and make decisions with depth and intention. And the best part? With practice, discernment becomes a habit, a natural part of how you navigate the world.

The Consequences of a Lack of Discernment

Before we dive deeper into how to build discernment, it's important to recognize the cost of not cultivating this skill. Without discernment, we can become reactive instead of intentional. We may find ourselves saying "yes" to commitments that drain us, pursuing goals that don't truly resonate, or trusting people who don't have our best interests at heart.

Consider these scenarios:

- You accept a promotion at work because it seems like the logical next step, only to realize months later that it's not aligned with your passions or strengths.

- You make a financial investment based on someone else's advice without fully understanding the risks, and it doesn't pan out.
- You stay in a relationship or friendship because of a sense of obligation, even though it no longer brings you joy or growth.

These experiences are common, but they're not inevitable. With discernment, you can navigate these situations more wisely and avoid unnecessary regret.

The Barriers to Discernment

Developing discernment isn't always easy. In fact, there are several barriers that can cloud our judgment and make it difficult to see clearly. Here are a few of the most common obstacles:

1. **Emotional Biases**
   Emotions are a natural and important part of decision-making, but they can also cloud our judgment. Fear, excitement, anger, or even guilt can lead us to make impulsive decisions that don't serve our long-term interests.
2. **Information Overload**
   In today's digital age, we're constantly bombarded with information. From social media to 24-hour news cycles, the sheer volume of input can overwhelm us, making it hard to filter out what's relevant and true.
3. **External Pressures**
   Society, culture, and even well-meaning friends and family often have opinions about what we should do. It's easy to get swept up in others' expectations and lose sight of our own values and desires.
4. **Fear of Uncertainty**
   Many people struggle with the discomfort of not knowing. This fear can push us to make decisions quickly, just to avoid sitting with ambiguity— even if rushing leads to poor outcomes.

5. **Ego and Pride**

Sometimes, our own ego can get in the way. We may cling to a decision because admitting we were wrong feels too difficult, or we might prioritize looking good over doing what's right.

By becoming aware of these barriers, we can begin to recognize when they're influencing us and take steps to overcome them.

The Role of Intuition, Logic, and Emotion

One of the keys to mastering discernment is understanding how to balance intuition, logic, and emotion in decision-making. Each of these elements plays a vital role, but relying too heavily on one can lead to imbalance.

- **Intuition:** This is the quiet, inner voice that guides you. Intuition often knows the answer before your conscious mind does, but it requires trust and practice to hear it clearly.
- **Logic:** Logic provides the structure and reasoning to evaluate options. It helps you weigh pros and cons, consider risks, and analyze facts. However, logic alone can sometimes overlook the human element.
- **Emotion:** Emotions bring color and depth to our decisions. They help us connect with our desires, values, and passions. Yet, emotions can also be fleeting and need to be tempered with reason.

The art of discernment lies in integrating these three elements, using them as complementary tools rather than competing forces.

A Framework for Discernment

To lay the foundation for your discernment practice, here's a simple framework you can start using right away:

1. **Pause:** When faced with a decision, resist the urge to act immediately. Give yourself space to reflect.
2. **Reflect:** Ask yourself key questions: What's driving this decision? Is it aligned with my values? What are the potential outcomes?
3. **Seek Clarity:** Identify any external pressures or biases that might be clouding your judgment.
4. **Decide:** Make your choice with intention, knowing that no decision is perfect but every decision is an opportunity to learn.
5. **Review:** Afterward, evaluate the outcome and the process. What worked? What didn't? What can you take into future decisions?

This framework is just the beginning. As you progress through this book, you'll learn how to deepen and refine each step, creating a discernment practice that feels natural and empowering.

Closing Reflection: You Will Get There

Discernment is not a destination; it's a journey. It's not about getting every decision right, but about learning and growing through the process of choosing. As you begin this journey, remember to be patient with yourself. Developing discernment takes time, but every small step you take will bring you closer to a life of clarity, alignment, and purpose.

2

The Mind-Heart Connection

The Harmony Between Mind and Heart

Discernment isn't purely a mental exercise. It's an intricate dance between the rational mind and the emotional heart. While the mind offers logic, analysis, and structure, the heart provides depth, meaning, and intuition. Both are essential to making wise decisions, but the challenge lies in balancing the two. When we rely too heavily on one and ignore the other, our decisions can feel unbalanced, misaligned, or incomplete.

This chapter explores the connection between mind and heart, showing you how to harness the strengths of both to strengthen your discernment skills. You'll discover how to recognize when your mind or heart is dominating your choices and learn techniques to create harmony between these two powerful forces.

The Role of the Mind: Logic, Reason, and Clarity

The mind is a brilliant tool for processing information and solving problems. It breaks down complex situations into manageable pieces, weighs pros and cons, and helps us anticipate outcomes. Without the mind's rationality, decision-making would feel chaotic and overwhelming.

However, the mind also has its limitations. It can be influenced by biases, overanalyze situations to the point of paralysis, or reduce deeply personal decisions to mere calculations. While logic is essential, discernment requires us to go beyond logic alone.

When the Mind Dominates

- You make decisions solely based on facts and data, ignoring feelings or intuition.
- You get stuck in "analysis paralysis," overthinking every detail and struggling to make a choice.
- You dismiss emotional or spiritual considerations as irrelevant or irrational.

The Strength of the Mind in Discernment

- Provides clarity by organizing thoughts and options.
- Helps identify potential risks and logical consequences.
- Balances emotions by bringing structure to the decision-making process.

The Role of the Heart: Emotion, Intuition, and Meaning

The heart represents our emotional and intuitive selves. It's where we connect with our values, desires, and inner wisdom. The heart allows us to feel deeply, to sense what truly resonates with us, and to choose paths that bring fulfillment and purpose.

But just like the mind, the heart has its pitfalls. If we allow emotions to dominate without tempering them with reason, we may act impulsively or make decisions driven by fleeting feelings rather than long-term alignment.

When the Heart Dominates

- You make decisions based solely on how you feel in the moment, without considering the bigger picture.
- You follow your intuition but ignore evidence or practical realities.
- You let fear, anger, or excitement drive impulsive choices.

The Strength of the Heart in Discernment

- Connects you to your deeper values and desires.
- Brings authenticity and meaning to your decisions.
- Allows you to tap into intuition, your inner compass for alignment.

The Power of Integrating Mind and Heart

True discernment lies in integrating the strengths of both mind and heart. When the two are in harmony, you can make decisions that are not only logical but also deeply aligned with who you are. You can weigh facts without losing sight of feelings, and you can trust your intuition while remaining grounded in reason.

Consider these scenarios:

1. You're offered a promotion at work. Your mind recognizes the financial and career benefits, but your heart senses that the role doesn't align with your passions. By integrating both perspectives, you can explore whether there's a way to accept the promotion while maintaining alignment or if it's better to pass.
2. You're deciding whether to end a long-term relationship. Your heart is attached to the memories and emotions, while your mind sees patterns of conflict and incompatibility. By balancing the two, you can assess whether the relationship can grow or whether it's time to move on.

In both cases, the integration of mind and heart leads to deeper discernment, allowing you to make choices that feel both logical and meaningful.

Techniques for Harmonizing Mind and Heart

To strengthen the connection between mind and heart, try these practices:

1. **Mindful Reflection**
   Before making a decision, take time to sit quietly and reflect. Ask yourself:

   What is my mind telling me about this situation?
   What is my heart telling me?
   Are they in agreement? If not, why?

   Write down your thoughts and feelings. Seeing them side by side can help you recognize where they align and where they conflict.

2. **The Head-Heart Alignment Exercise**
   Close your eyes and take a few deep breaths.

   Place one hand on your forehead (representing the mind) and the other on your chest (representing the heart).

   Focus on the decision at hand. Ask your mind, *"What do you think?"* Then ask your heart, *"What do you feel?"*

   Listen to both responses without judgment. Reflect on how they can work together.

3. **The 10-10-10 Rule**
   This simple tool helps balance emotions with long-term thinking. Ask yourself:

How will I feel about this decision 10 minutes from now?
How will I feel 10 months from now?
How will I feel 10 years from now?

This exercise allows the mind to consider long-term consequences while giving the heart space to weigh emotional significance.

4. **Meditation and Visualization**
   Practice meditation to quiet mental chatter and connect with your inner self.

   Use visualization to imagine the outcomes of each decision. Which path feels lighter, more aligned, and truer to who you are?

5. **Seek Feedback from Trusted Sources**
   When you're struggling to integrate mind and heart, seek input from someone you trust. Share both your logical thoughts and emotional feelings, and ask for their perspective. Sometimes an outside voice can help you see the balance you're missing.

Learning to Trust the Process

Harmonizing mind and heart takes time and practice. You may not always get it right, and that's okay. Each decision is an opportunity to refine your discernment skills. Over time, you'll find that integrating mind and heart becomes second nature, empowering you to make choices that feel both clear and deeply aligned.

As you continue this journey, remember that discernment is not about eliminating uncertainty; it's about navigating it with wisdom and grace. The more you listen to both your mind and heart, the more confident and aligned your decisions will become.

Closing Reflection: The Mind / Heart Partnership

The mind and heart are not rivals; they are partners. Together, they form a powerful foundation for discernment. By learning to balance logic and emotion, analysis and intuition, you can approach every decision with clarity, authenticity, and purpose. Trust in the connection between your mind and heart, it is the key to living a life of wise, intentional choices.

3

Values, Vision, and Alignment

The Compass of Discernment

Imagine trying to navigate a journey without a map or compass. You'd wander aimlessly, unsure of whether you're heading toward your destination or farther away. This is what decision-making feels like when we lack a clear understanding of our values and vision. Our values are our internal compass, pointing us toward what matters most, while our vision is the map, outlining where we want to go. Together, they guide us toward alignment, a state where our decisions and actions reflect who we truly are.

This chapter is about uncovering and clarifying your values and vision so that you can make decisions with confidence and purpose. By understanding what truly matters to you and where you want to go, you can create a foundation for discernment that ensures your choices lead to a life of alignment and fulfillment.

What Are Values, and Why Do They Matter?

Values are the principles and beliefs that define what is important to you. They are deeply personal and may stem from your upbringing, culture, experiences, or aspirations. Values are not just abstract concepts; they influence every decision you make, whether you realize it or not.

For example:

- If you value **family**, you might prioritize spending time with loved ones over pursuing a career that requires constant travel.
- If you value **creativity**, you might seek opportunities that allow you to express yourself rather than settling for routine work.
- If you value **integrity**, you'll likely choose honesty, even when it's uncomfortable.

Without clarity on your values, it's easy to feel conflicted or directionless. When you understand and honor your values, you gain a powerful tool for discernment.

Exercise: Discovering Your Core Values

Take a moment to reflect on the following questions:

1. What brings you the greatest sense of fulfillment or joy?
2. What causes or issues stir your passion or anger?
3. Think of a time when you felt completely at peace. What were you doing? Who were you with?
4. What qualities do you admire most in others?
5. When faced with a tough decision, what principles guide you?

Write down the answers and look for patterns or recurring themes. From these, identify your top 3–5 core values. These are the guiding principles that can anchor your decision-making process.

Vision: Charting Your Path

While values ground you, your vision propels you forward. Vision is the ability to imagine the future you desire, a clear picture of who you want to become and the life you want to create. Without vision, decisions can feel random or reactive. With vision, they become stepping stones toward a meaningful destination.

What Does an Aligned Vision Look Like?

Your vision doesn't have to be grand or perfect, but it should feel authentic and inspiring. It might include goals for your:

- **Career**: What kind of work excites you? What legacy do you want to leave?
- **Relationships**: What kind of connections bring you joy and growth?
- **Health**: How do you want to feel physically and mentally?
- **Personal growth**: What skills, knowledge, or experiences do you want to gain?
- **Contribution**: How do you want to make a difference in the world?

Your vision can be broad or detailed, but it should align with your core values and reflect your unique aspirations.

Exercise: Crafting Your Vision Statement

1. Close your eyes and imagine your ideal life 5–10 years from now. Where are you? What are you doing? Who are you with?
2. Write down your answers, focusing on how you want to feel rather than specific achievements.
3. Summarize your vision in a single, inspiring statement. For example: *"I envision a life where I am creating meaningful art, surrounded by supportive relationships, and contributing to my community."*

"I see myself thriving in a career that challenges me intellectually, while maintaining balance with my family and personal well-being."

Your vision statement will serve as a guidepost for your decisions, helping you evaluate whether each choice brings you closer to or further from your desired future.

Alignment: Bridging Values and Vision

Alignment occurs when your decisions, actions, and goals are consistent with your values and vision. It's the sweet spot where your inner world (what you believe and desire) matches your outer world (what you do and create). When you're in alignment, life feels purposeful and fulfilling. When you're out of alignment, you may feel stuck, conflicted, or restless.

Signs of Alignment:

- You feel energized and motivated by your daily activities.
- You experience fewer regrets or second-guessing.
- Your decisions feel "right," even if they're challenging.
- You sense a deep connection between who you are and what you do.

Signs of Misalignment:

- You feel drained or uninspired by your routines.
- You frequently question whether you're on the right path.
- You make decisions based on fear, pressure, or external expectations.
- You experience a disconnect between your actions and your deeper desires.

Bringing It All Together: Using Values and Vision to Guide Discernment

Once you've identified your core values and vision, you can use them as tools for discernment. When faced with a decision, ask yourself:

1. **Does this align with my values?**
   For example, if you value honesty, is this choice truthful? If you value balance, will this decision disrupt your equilibrium?
2. **Does this move me closer to my vision?**
   Will this choice bring you closer to your desired future, or is it a distraction?
3. **Am I honoring my authentic self?**
   Is this decision rooted in what *you* want, or are you influenced by societal norms, peer pressure, or fear?

Exercise: The Alignment Check-In

1. Write down a current decision you're struggling with.
2. List your top values and your vision statement.
3. For each value, ask: Does this decision honor this value? Why or why not?
4. Consider your vision: Does this choice align with where I want to go?

Reflect on your answers. If the decision aligns with your values and vision, it's likely a wise choice. If it doesn't, it may be worth reconsidering.

Closing Reflection: Living in Alignment

Clarifying your values and vision is not a one-time task, it's an ongoing process. As you grow and evolve, your priorities may shift, and that's okay. The key is to regularly check in with yourself, ensuring your decisions reflect your authentic self.

When you live in alignment, you'll find that discernment becomes easier and more natural. Your values act as a compass, your vision serves as a map, and alignment bridges the two. Together, they empower you to navigate life with confidence, clarity, and purpose.

Take a moment to review your values and vision now. Write them down and keep them somewhere visible. Let them guide you as you move forward. With these tools, you're building the foundation for a life that feels true to who you are.

4

The Power of Pause

The Gift of Stillness

In today's fast-paced world, we often feel pressure to act quickly. Deadlines loom, notifications ping, and there's always a sense that we need to make decisions *now*. But one of the most powerful tools in the practice of discernment is the ability to pause.

Pausing is not procrastination, nor is it avoidance. It's an intentional act of stepping back to create space for clarity and reflection. When we pause, we interrupt the autopilot mode of reacting and give ourselves the opportunity to respond thoughtfully. It's in this stillness that true discernment begins.

This chapter explores the importance of pausing, why it's so effective, and how you can incorporate it into your daily life. You'll learn techniques to slow down, even in the busiest moments, and discover how this simple act can transform the quality of your decisions.

Why We Struggle to Pause

In a culture that values speed and productivity, pausing can feel counter-intuitive. We may fear that taking a moment to reflect will make us seem indecisive or that we'll miss opportunities if we don't act quickly. But this mindset often leads to rushed decisions and regrets.

Here are some common reasons why we struggle to pause:

1. **Fear of Missing Out (FOMO):** We worry that by waiting, we'll lose out on an opportunity.
2. **External Pressure:** Deadlines and expectations from others push us to act before we're ready.
3. **Discomfort with Stillness:** For many, silence or stillness feels uncomfortable, leading to a compulsion to "do something."
4. **Cultural Conditioning:** We're taught to equate busyness with success, leaving little room for reflection.

Recognizing these barriers is the first step to overcoming them. Pausing isn't about wasting time; it's about reclaiming control over your choices.

The Benefits of Pausing

Pausing before making a decision offers several profound benefits:

1. **Clarity:** Stepping back allows you to see the situation more clearly, free from the haze of stress or urgency.
2. **Emotional Regulation:** Pausing gives you time to process emotions, preventing reactive or impulsive decisions.
3. **Perspective:** When you pause, you can consider multiple viewpoints and long-term consequences.
4. **Alignment:** Reflection ensures that your choice aligns with your values and vision.

5. **Improved Outcomes:** Decisions made with care and intention are more likely to lead to positive results.

Techniques for Practicing the Pause

Here are practical strategies to help you develop the habit of pausing, even in high-pressure situations:

1. **Take a Deep Breath**
   When faced with a decision, pause for a moment and take a deep breath. This simple act helps calm your nervous system, reduces stress, and creates a moment of stillness. Repeat the process as needed until you feel centered.

2. **Ask for Time**
   If someone is pressuring you for an answer, it's okay to say, "Let me think about it and get back to you." This gives you the space to reflect without making a rushed decision.

3. **Set a Rule for Big Decisions**
   For significant decisions, such as changing jobs, making a major purchase, or ending a relationship, create a personal rule to pause for a specific amount of time (e.g., 24 hours, a week). This ensures you're not acting impulsively.

4. **Create a Ritual of Reflection**
   Incorporate regular pauses into your day. This could be a morning meditation, an evening journaling session, or simply a five-minute break to sit quietly and reflect.

5. **Use the STOP Method**
   The STOP method is a mindfulness technique that helps you pause and ground yourself in the present moment:
   S: Stop what you're doing.
   T: Take a breath.
   O: Observe your thoughts, feelings, and surroundings.
   P: Proceed with intention.

6. **Visualize the Future**

   When you pause, take a moment to visualize the possible outcomes of your decision. Imagine how each choice might play out and how it aligns with your values and vision.

Pausing in High-Stakes Situations

It's one thing to pause when you're alone and have plenty of time, but what about when you're in the middle of a high-stakes or high-pressure situation? Here are some tips for pausing in these moments:

1. **Ground Yourself**: Focus on your breath or a physical sensation (e.g., your feet on the ground) to anchor yourself in the present.
2. **Repeat a Mantra**: Use a calming phrase like "I have time" or "Let me think" to create mental space.
3. **Buy Time**: If possible, delay the decision, even by a few minutes, to give yourself a moment to reflect.
4. **Consult Your Inner Voice**: Ask yourself, "What feels right in this moment?" before responding.

The Courage to Pause

Pausing takes courage, especially in a society that values quick answers and constant activity. It requires you to trust yourself and the process of discernment, even when others expect immediate action. But as you practice pausing, you'll find that it's not a weakness—it's a strength.

When you pause, you reclaim your power. You step out of reactive patterns and into intentional living. You create space for wisdom, clarity, and alignment to guide your decisions. And over time, you'll notice a shift—not just in the quality of your choices, but in the overall rhythm and flow of your life.

Reflection Exercise: The Power of Pause in Action

1. Think of a recent decision you made that didn't turn out as you'd hoped.
2. Reflect on whether you paused before making the decision. Did you rush into it? What influenced your choice?
3. Now imagine how pausing might have changed the outcome. What would you have done differently?

This exercise will help you recognize the value of pausing and inspire you to incorporate it into future decisions.

Closing Reflection: Pausing as a Way of Life

The power of pause is more than a strategy for decision-making—it's a mindset and a way of life. By cultivating the habit of pausing, you'll find yourself navigating life with greater calm, clarity, and confidence.

Remember, you don't need to have all the answers immediately. Taking the time to pause and reflect is not a sign of indecision; it's a sign of wisdom. The next time you face a choice, big or small, give yourself the gift of stillness. Pause, breathe, and trust that clarity will come.

As you move forward, keep practicing the pause. It's a small act with a big impact; one that will transform not only your decisions but also the way you experience life itself.

5

Listening to Your Inner Voice

The Quiet Power of Intuition

Within each of us lies a quiet, steady voice that often knows the answer before we do. This is your inner voice, *your intuition*. It's not loud or insistent, like the chatter of your mind. Instead, it's subtle and calm, guiding you toward alignment with your truest self. Yet, in the noise of everyday life, this voice is often drowned out by external opinions, fears, and doubts.

Listening to your inner voice is one of the most profound skills in discernment. It allows you to tap into a deeper well of wisdom, one that goes beyond logic and emotion. This chapter explores how to recognize, trust, and strengthen your connection with your intuition so you can make decisions that feel authentic and aligned.

What Is Your Inner Voice?

Your inner voice (or intuition) is your subconscious mind's way of communicating insights to you. It's the result of accumulated experiences, knowledge, and observations that your conscious mind may not fully process. Intuition bridges the gap between the rational and the spiritual, offering a holistic perspective that logic alone can't provide.

Unlike fear or anxiety, which are driven by worry about the future, your inner voice is grounded and nonjudgmental. It doesn't shout or demand—it whispers truths that resonate deeply within you. Learning to recognize and trust this voice is key to cultivating discernment.

How Intuition Communicates

Your inner voice may manifest in different ways, such as:

- A gut feeling or physical sensation (e.g., a sense of unease or warmth).
- A sudden insight or clarity about a situation.
- A feeling of resonance or dissonance when considering a choice.
- A subtle "knowing" that you can't fully explain.

Recognizing these signals requires mindfulness and self-awareness, which we'll explore further in this chapter.

Why We Ignore Our Inner Voice

Many of us struggle to hear or trust our intuition. Here's why:

1. **Noise and Distractions:** Modern life is filled with distractions that drown out our inner voice. Constant stimulation from technology, media, and social obligations leaves little room for introspection.
2. **External Opinions:** We often prioritize the advice and expectations of others over our own instincts. This can lead to second-guessing ourselves or ignoring what we truly feel.
3. **Fear of Mistakes:** Trusting your inner voice requires courage. Fear of making the "wrong" decision can cause us to rely solely on logic or external validation.
4. **Overthinking:** When we over-analyze a situation, we can lose touch

with our intuitive sense. Intuition thrives in stillness, not in mental clutter.

Strengthening Your Connection to Your Inner Voice

Developing the ability to hear and trust your intuition takes practice, but it's a skill anyone can cultivate. Here are techniques to help you tune in to your inner voice:

1. **Practice Stillness**
   Intuition speaks in moments of quiet. Create space for stillness in your daily routine, whether through meditation, deep breathing, or simply sitting in silence. Let your thoughts settle and notice what arises.
2. **Journal Your Thoughts**
   Writing down your thoughts and feelings can help you uncover intuitive insights. When faced with a decision, try freewriting; let your thoughts flow onto the page without judgment. You may find clarity hidden in your words.
3. **Pay Attention to Physical Sensations**
   Your body often reacts to your intuition before your mind does. Notice how you feel physically when considering a decision. Does your chest feel tight? Does your stomach feel calm? These signals can offer valuable guidance.
4. **Ask Open-Ended Questions**
   Pose questions to your inner voice and listen for the answers. For example:

   "What choice feels most aligned with my values?"
   "What am I not seeing in this situation?"
   "What would bring me peace?"

You may not get an immediate answer, but with patience, clarity will come.

5. **Follow Small Nudges**

   Trusting your inner voice starts with small acts of faith. Begin by listening to your intuition in low-stakes situations, like choosing what to eat or which route to take. As you build confidence in these small choices, you'll find it easier to trust your intuition in bigger decisions.

Distinguishing Intuition from Fear or Impulse

One of the challenges of trusting your inner voice is distinguishing it from fear, anxiety, or impulsive desires. Here's how to tell the difference:

- **Intuition is calm:** It feels like a steady "knowing," not a frantic urge or worry.
- **Fear is loud:** It often involves "what if" scenarios and a sense of urgency.
- **Intuition is grounded:** It aligns with your values and long-term vision.
- **Impulse is fleeting:** It's driven by immediate gratification or reaction.

When in doubt, take a moment to pause and reflect. Ask yourself, "Is this decision coming from a place of wisdom or fear?" Trust that your intuition will guide you if you give it space to emerge.

Overcoming Doubts About Intuition

It's natural to question your inner voice, especially if you've ignored it in the past or made decisions you regret. But intuition is like a muscle; the more you use it, the stronger it becomes. Here are ways to build trust in your inner voice:

1. **Reflect on Past Decisions**

   Think of a time when you followed your intuition. What was the outcome? Now think of a time when you ignored it. What happened? These reflections can help you recognize the wisdom of your inner voice.

2. **Be Patient with Yourself**

Learning to trust your intuition takes time. Even if you make mistakes along the way, view them as opportunities to refine your discernment.

3. **Celebrate Small Wins**

   When you follow your intuition and it leads to a positive outcome, acknowledge it. Celebrating these moments reinforces your confidence in your inner voice.

Exercise: Intuition Journaling

1. Think of a decision you're currently facing.
2. Write down the options you're considering.
3. Close your eyes, take a deep breath, and ask yourself: *"What feels right in my heart?"*
4. Write down your immediate thoughts, feelings, or impressions without overthinking.
5. Review your answers. What insights emerged?

This exercise helps you access your intuitive sense and trust the guidance it provides.

Closing Reflection: Trust the Whisper Within

Your inner voice is one of the most powerful tools in the practice of discernment. It's always there, quietly guiding you toward choices that align with your deepest truths. While it may take time and practice to hear and trust this voice, the effort is worth it. Intuition doesn't guarantee a life free from mistakes, but it offers a path that feels authentic and deeply aligned with who you are.

As you move forward, commit to creating space for your inner voice. Practice stillness, listen to your instincts, and trust the wisdom within you. With time, you'll find that this quiet voice becomes a trusted guide, helping you navigate life with clarity, courage, and grace.

6

Seeking Wise Counsel

The Balance Between Self-Reliance and External Guidance

No one makes decisions in isolation. Whether we realize it or not, our choices are often influenced by the opinions, advice, and experiences of others. While listening to your inner voice is vital, seeking wise counsel is equally important. Trusted mentors, friends, or advisors can provide new perspectives, challenge your assumptions, and help you see blind spots that your intuition or logic alone might miss.

But not all advice is created equal. One of the keys to discernment is learning to identify the right people to seek counsel from and understanding how to weigh their input without losing sight of your own values and vision. This chapter will help you develop the skills to ask for and evaluate external advice effectively, while staying true to yourself.

The Role of Others in the Discernment Process

When you seek counsel from others, you're inviting them into your decision-making process. This can be incredibly valuable, as it brings:

1. **Perspective:** Others may see the situation differently, offering insights you hadn't considered.
2. **Experience:** People who have faced similar challenges can share lessons learned and potential pitfalls.
3. **Support:** Knowing you're not alone in your decision can provide emotional reassurance and clarity.

However, it's essential to remember that advice from others is not a substitute for your own judgment. Rather, it's a tool to complement your discernment process.

Choosing the Right People for Counsel

Not everyone's advice is helpful, and seeking input from the wrong people can lead to confusion or misguided decisions. Here are some qualities to look for when choosing someone to guide you:

1. **Trustworthiness:** Choose someone who has your best interests at heart and can provide honest feedback.
2. **Experience or Expertise:** Seek counsel from individuals with knowledge or experience relevant to your situation.
3. **Objectivity:** Look for people who can provide unbiased advice without imposing their own agenda or emotions.
4. **Alignment with Your Values:** Choose someone whose principles align with your own, ensuring their advice resonates with your core beliefs.
5. **Empathy and Respect:** A good advisor listens to you and respects your autonomy, rather than dictating what you "should" do.

Who Not to Seek Advice From:

- People who have a history of being overly critical or judgmental.
- Those who are emotionally invested in the outcome and may have their own biases.

- Individuals who tend to project their own fears or insecurities onto others.

How to Seek Wise Counsel Effectively

Once you've identified the right people, the way you approach them can make a big difference in the quality of the advice you receive. Here are some strategies to help you seek counsel effectively:

1. **Be Clear About Your Needs**
   Before reaching out, clarify what you're seeking: Are you looking for practical solutions, emotional support, or simply a sounding board? Communicate this clearly to the person you're asking for advice.

   Example: "I'm considering changing careers and could use your perspective since you've made a similar transition. I'd like to hear about your experience and any advice you might have."

2. **Frame the Situation Objectively**
   Present the facts of your situation without exaggerating or omitting details. This helps the other person provide balanced, thoughtful advice. Avoid leading questions that push them toward a specific answer.

   Example: Instead of saying, "Don't you think I should quit my job because it's awful?" try, "I've been feeling unfulfilled in my current job and am considering a change. Here's why. What are your thoughts?"

3. **Be Open to Feedback**
   When you seek counsel, be prepared to hear things you might not want to hear. Wise counsel often challenges your assumptions or highlights areas you've overlooked. Approach the conversation with curiosity and a willingness to learn.

4. **Ask Specific Questions**

General advice can be vague or unhelpful. Ask specific questions to get targeted insights. For example:

"What do you think are the biggest risks of this decision?"
"Do you see any blind spots I might be missing?"
"Based on your experience, what would you recommend I consider?"

5. **Take Responsibility for the Final Decision**

Remember, the purpose of seeking counsel is to inform your discernment, not to let others decide for you. After gathering input, take time to reflect and weigh it against your own intuition, values, and vision.

Evaluating the Advice You Receive

Not all advice is useful, even when it comes from trusted sources. Here's how to evaluate the input you receive:

1. **Consider the Source**

Ask yourself: Does this person have the experience, knowledge, or perspective to offer meaningful advice in this situation? Are they coming from a place of genuine care and objectivity?

2. **Filter for Bias**

Recognize that even well-meaning people may have biases based on their own experiences, fears, or desires. For example, someone who regrets taking risks in their life might advise you to play it safe, even if that's not the best choice for you.

3. **Assess Alignment with Your Values and Vision**

Does the advice resonate with your core values and long-term goals? If not, it may be worth considering alternative perspectives.

4. **Look for Patterns**

If you've sought counsel from multiple people, pay attention to recurring themes or consistent advice. This can help you identify the most relevant insights.

5. **Trust Your Inner Voice**

   Ultimately, you are the one living with the consequences of your decision. After reflecting on the advice you've received, tune back in to your inner voice to determine what feels right for you.

The Balance Between Advice and Autonomy

Seeking wise counsel doesn't mean giving away your power. It's about gathering insights while maintaining ownership of your choices. Here are some tips for balancing external advice with your own discernment:

- **Anchor Yourself First:** Before seeking advice, take time to reflect on your own thoughts and feelings. This ensures you're not overly swayed by others.
- **Use Advice as a Mirror, Not a Blueprint:** Let advice reflect new possibilities or blind spots, but don't feel obligated to follow it exactly.
- **Express Gratitude:** Even if you choose not to follow someone's advice, thank them for their time and perspective.

Exercise: The Circle of Counsel

1. Identify 3–5 people in your life whom you trust to provide wise counsel. Write their names and note their strengths or areas of expertise.
2. Reflect on a current decision you're facing. Who in this circle might offer the most helpful perspective?
3. Reach out to that person, using the techniques discussed in this chapter.

This exercise helps you build a reliable support network while practicing the skill of seeking and evaluating advice.

Closing Reflection: The Value of Shared Wisdom

Wise counsel is one of the most valuable resources in the discernment process. By inviting trusted individuals into your journey, you gain access to new perspectives, insights, and support. Yet, the ultimate responsibility for your decisions lies with you. As you learn to balance external guidance with your own inner voice, you'll find yourself making choices that are not only informed but also deeply aligned with your authentic self.

The art of discernment is a collaborative process, one that honors both your independence and your connection to others. By seeking wise counsel intentionally and thoughtfully, you'll strengthen your ability to navigate life's complexities with clarity and confidence.

7

The Power of Perception - Understanding Other's Motives

What Lies Beneath the Surface?

Every day, we make decisions that are influenced consciously or unconsciously by the motives of those around us. A friend gives us advice, a boss offers an opportunity, a family member makes a request. On the surface, these interactions may seem straightforward, but beneath them lie motives, some genuine, some self-serving, and some a complex mix of both.

Discernment is not just about what decision to make; it's also about who is influencing that decision and why. Understanding others' motives allows us to:

- Distinguish genuine support from hidden agendas
- Recognize when we are being manipulated or misled
- Protect ourselves from bias, misinformation, or undue pressure
- Build trustworthy relationships based on authenticity

This chapter will explore how to read between the lines, question what's not being said, and apply discernment in navigating external influences.

The Spectrum of Motives – From Altruism to Self-Interest

Not all motives are bad, but not all are pure either. People's actions are driven by a mix of:

- **Altruism:** Acting for the good of others without expecting anything in return.
- **Mutual Benefit:** A decision that benefits both parties.
- **Personal Gain:** Prioritizing one's own interests over others.
- **Manipulation:** Deception or persuasion to serve a selfish purpose.

For example:

- A mentor offering career advice may genuinely want to help, but may also subconsciously steer you toward choices that reflect their own values and experiences.
- A friend encouraging you to make a big move may support your dreams, or they may fear being left behind and subtly discourage you from pursuing new opportunities.
- A boss offering a promotion may value your work, or they may see you as someone who will take on extra responsibility without questioning it.

By learning to recognize where motives fall on this spectrum, we can make clearer, more informed choices.

Identifying Underlying Motives

What's Not Being Said?

Often, it's not what people say that reveals their true motives; it's what they leave out. Hidden motives can be detected by:

- **Observing inconsistencies**: Does their advice change depending on their own situation?
- **Paying attention to hesitation**: Do they avoid giving direct answers?
- **Noting emotional pressure**: Are they using guilt or urgency to push you toward a decision?

Emotional Appeals vs. Logical Reasoning

- Are they making emotional arguments ("Do this because it will make me happy") or logical ones ("This is why it aligns with your goals")?
- Do you feel pushed toward a decision quickly?
- Does their tone suggest genuine care or subtle control?

The Benefit Question

A simple way to discern motives is to ask: *Who benefits from this decision?*

- If the answer is only them, proceed with caution.
- If it benefits both of you fairly, it may be worth considering.

If it benefits you more than them, assess whether they are truly being selfless or if there is an unspoken expectation of reciprocity.

Evaluating Advice: The Motives Behind Guidance

Seeking guidance is essential, but not all advice is free from bias. Before accepting someone's input, ask yourself:

1. What is their experience or expertise in this area?
2. Do they have a personal stake in my decision?
3. Are they imposing their own fears or biases onto me?
4. Are they encouraging me to think critically or simply telling me what to do?

Example 1:

A family member discourages you from starting a business because they believe it's "too risky." Is this based on their own fears or actual financial knowledge?

Example 2:

A mentor tells you to take a leadership role even though you're unsure if it's right for you. Are they pushing you because they see your potential, or because they want credit for shaping your success?

By filtering advice through these questions, you can distill wisdom from bias.

Applying This to Key Areas of Life

Relationships

- Recognizing when someone genuinely supports you versus wants to control you.
- Understanding when emotional appeals are rooted in care or meant to manipulate.

Career & Workplace

- Identifying office politics and hidden agendas in promotions or assignments.
- Recognizing when feedback is constructive versus designed to undermine confidence.

Financial Decisions

- Evaluating sales pitches and financial offers—are they in your best interest or someone else's?

- Noticing when pressure tactics are used to push you into a purchase.

Spiritual & Ethical Choices

- Being aware of how religious, cultural, or ethical viewpoints may be used to influence your decisions.
- Understanding when a cause aligns with your values versus when it's being used to manipulate emotions.

Practical Strategies for Seeing Through Motives

1. **Ask Direct Questions** – When someone gives advice or a request, ask:
   "Why do you think this is the best option for me?"
   "What would you do if you were in my situation?"
2. **Observe Actions, Not Just Words** – People's behaviors over time reveal more than what they say.
3. **Avoid Emotional Pressure** – Take a step back before making decisions under stress, guilt, or urgency.
4. **Test Integrity Over Time** – Trust should be built gradually. Repeated patterns tell you everything.
5. **Use a Neutral Third-Party Perspective** – Get advice from someone with no personal stake in the outcome.

Closing Reflection: Balancing Skepticism with Openness

Understanding motives is not about becoming distrustful or assuming bad intent, it's about practicing awareness. When we take others' motives into account, we:

- Make decisions from a place of clarity rather than manipulation.
- Develop healthier relationships with trust and respect.
- Protect ourselves from undue influence while remaining open to wisdom.

By integrating this skill into daily life, discernment becomes not just about what is right for us, but also about who we allow to shape our choices.

8

Discernment in Relationships

The Foundation of Connection

Our relationships shape every aspect of our lives. They influence our happiness, growth, and sense of belonging. Whether it's with a partner, family member, friend, or colleague, relationships require ongoing decisions about how we invest our time, energy, and trust. Practicing discernment in relationships allows us to build connections that are healthy, fulfilling, and aligned with our values.

This chapter will explore how to use discernment to navigate the complexities of relationships, including recognizing healthy and unhealthy dynamics, setting boundaries, and making thoughtful choices about who to let into your life. By applying the principles of discernment to your relationships, you can foster deeper connections while protecting your emotional well-being.

Understanding Healthy vs. Unhealthy Relationships

The first step in practicing discernment in relationships is learning to recognize the difference between healthy and unhealthy dynamics. While no relationship is perfect, healthy connections are characterized by mutual respect, trust, and support, whereas unhealthy ones often involve control, manipulation, or emotional harm.

Signs of a Healthy Relationship:

- Open and honest communication.
- Mutual respect for boundaries and individuality.
- A balance of giving and receiving support.
- Encouragement for personal growth and self-expression.
- The ability to navigate conflicts constructively.

Signs of an Unhealthy Relationship:

- Frequent criticism, blame, or belittling.
- Lack of trust or consistent dishonesty.
- Controlling behavior or a lack of respect for boundaries.
- Emotional manipulation or guilt-tripping.
- Feeling drained, anxious, or unsupported after interactions.

Recognizing these patterns is an essential part of discernment, as it allows you to evaluate whether a relationship is contributing to or detracting from your overall well-being.

Questions to Guide Relationship Discernment

When evaluating a relationship, ask yourself the following questions to gain clarity about its dynamics:

1. **Does this relationship align with my values?**
   Are the core principles of this relationship (e.g., honesty, respect, reciprocity) consistent with your personal values?

2. **Does this person bring out the best in me?**
   Do you feel supported, encouraged, and free to be yourself, or do you feel diminished or constrained?

3. **Is there balance in this relationship?**
   Is there a healthy give-and-take, or is one person consistently giving while the other takes?

4. **How do I feel after spending time with this person?**
   Do you feel energized, valued, and connected, or do you feel drained, anxious, or unworthy?

5. **Can we navigate conflict respectfully?**
   Healthy relationships don't avoid conflict but handle it with mutual respect and a willingness to understand each other's perspectives.

Reflecting on these questions can help you discern whether a relationship is worth investing in or whether it needs adjustment—or even an exit.

Setting Boundaries with Discernment

Boundaries are a cornerstone of healthy relationships. They define what behavior is acceptable to you and protect your emotional and physical well-being. Practicing discernment in relationships means knowing when and how to set boundaries, as well as recognizing when boundaries are being crossed.

Steps to Setting Boundaries:

1. **Identify Your Limits:** Reflect on what behaviors make you feel uncomfortable, disrespected, or unsafe. These are areas where boundaries are needed.

2. **Communicate Clearly:** Express your boundaries in a calm and

respectful way. Be direct about your needs and expectations. For example, "I need time to recharge after work, so I'd appreciate it if we could talk later in the evening."

3. **Be Consistent:** Enforcing boundaries requires consistency. If someone repeatedly crosses a boundary, calmly remind them of your limit.

4. **Evaluate Their Response:** Pay attention to how the other person reacts to your boundaries. Do they respect them, or do they dismiss or challenge them?

When Boundaries Are Crossed:

If someone continues to disregard your boundaries despite clear communication, it may be a sign of an unhealthy dynamic. In these cases, discernment helps you decide whether to adjust your expectations, distance yourself, or end the relationship.

Navigating Toxic Relationships

Toxic relationships can be particularly challenging to navigate because they often involve emotional entanglement and manipulation. Discernment is critical in identifying toxic dynamics and deciding how to address them.

Signs of a Toxic Relationship:

- Constant negativity, criticism, or belittling.
- Gaslighting or denial of your experiences.
- Exploitation of your time, energy, or resources.
- Patterns of control, jealousy, or possessiveness.
- Repeated cycles of conflict and reconciliation without resolution.

Steps for Addressing Toxicity:

1. **Acknowledge the Reality:** Be honest with yourself about the unhealthy patterns in the relationship.
2. **Seek Support:** Talk to a trusted friend, counselor, or mentor to gain perspective and guidance.
3. **Set Firm Boundaries:** Communicate your limits clearly and consistently.
4. **Decide on the Future:** Use discernment to evaluate whether the relationship can change or whether it's time to let go.

Letting Go with Grace:

Ending a toxic relationship can be difficult, but it's often necessary for your growth and well-being. Focus on the lessons you've learned and the clarity you've gained, and allow yourself time to heal.

Investing in Meaningful Connections

While discernment helps you navigate challenges in relationships, it's also a tool for fostering meaningful connections. Use discernment to identify and nurture relationships that bring joy, growth, and mutual support.

How to Invest in Healthy Relationships:

1. **Be Present:** Show up fully for the people who matter to you. Listen actively, express appreciation, and prioritize quality time.
2. **Communicate Openly:** Share your thoughts, feelings, and needs honestly while inviting the same from others.
3. **Celebrate Growth:** Encourage each other's personal and shared growth. Celebrate successes and support each other during challenges.
4. **Reciprocate Effort:** Ensure there's a balance of giving and receiving, where both parties contribute to the relationship.

5. **Show Gratitude:** Acknowledge the value the other person brings to your life. Small gestures of gratitude can strengthen bonds.

Discernment in Different Types of Relationships

Discernment plays a unique role in different types of relationships:

- **Romantic Relationships:** Use discernment to choose a partner who aligns with your values, respects your boundaries, and supports your growth. Evaluate whether the relationship fosters mutual love and trust.
- **Friendships:** Invest in friendships that are reciprocal and uplifting. Use discernment to distance yourself from friendships that feel one-sided or draining.
- **Family Relationships:** While family bonds are important, discernment helps you navigate complex dynamics. Set boundaries where needed and prioritize your well-being.
- **Professional Relationships:** Discernment in the workplace helps you identify trustworthy colleagues, build constructive partnerships, and navigate office politics with integrity.

Reflection Exercise: Evaluating Your Relationships

1. Make a list of the key relationships in your life.
2. For each relationship, reflect on the following:

   How does this relationship make me feel?
   Does this person align with my values?
   Is this relationship balanced and supportive?

3. Identify one relationship that feels healthy and one that feels challenging. Consider how you can invest more in the healthy connection and what changes might be needed in the challenging one.

Closing Reflection: Choosing Connection with Intention

Relationships are at the heart of a meaningful life, and practicing discernment allows you to approach them with intention and wisdom. By recognizing healthy dynamics, setting boundaries, and letting go of toxic connections, you create space for relationships that nourish and inspire you.

As you continue to develop discernment in your relationships, remember to balance external advice with your own intuition and values. Whether it's a romantic partner, a lifelong friend, or a colleague, the quality of your connections will reflect the care and thoughtfulness you bring to them.

9

Discernment in Career and Finances

Building a Life of Purpose and Stability

For many of us, our careers and finances play a central role in how we structure our lives and achieve our goals. Yet, these areas are also sources of some of the most challenging and impactful decisions we'll ever make. Choosing the right career path, negotiating job offers, managing investments, and budgeting wisely all require discernment. Without it, we risk making choices based on fear, external pressure, or fleeting desires rather than alignment with our values and long-term vision.

This chapter focuses on how to bring discernment into your professional life and financial decision-making. You'll learn how to evaluate opportunities, set priorities, and create a career and financial strategy that supports your goals and values. By applying discernment in these areas, you can build a life that feels both purposeful and stable.

Discernment in Career Choices

Understanding Career Alignment

Your career is more than just a job; it's a significant part of how you express your skills, passions, and purpose. Practicing discernment in your career means evaluating not just the financial and professional benefits of a role, but also its alignment with your values, goals, and vision for your life.

Key Questions for Career Discernment:

1. **Does this role align with my values?** Does the company's mission, culture, and expectations resonate with what matters most to you?
2. **Does this role utilize my strengths and passions?** Will this job allow you to use your natural talents and engage in work you enjoy?
3. **Does this role support my long-term vision?** Will this position help you move closer to your personal and professional goals?
4. **How does this role impact my well-being?** Consider the work-life balance, stress levels, and overall fit with your lifestyle.

Evaluating Opportunities with Discernment

When considering a new job, promotion, or career pivot, discernment can help you make thoughtful decisions. Here's how to approach career opportunities with clarity:

1. **Assess the Opportunity:** Research the organization's values, culture, and reputation.
   Consider the role's responsibilities, growth potential, and how they align with your goals. Evaluate the financial package, benefits, and other practical factors.
2. **Reflect on Your Motivations:** Are you drawn to this opportunity because it aligns with your vision, or are you motivated by fear, external

pressure, or ego? Reflect on whether this choice is coming from a place of authenticity.

3. **Take Your Time:** Rushed decisions often lead to regret. If possible, take time to thoroughly evaluate the opportunity, seek advice, and tune into your inner voice.

4. **Consult Trusted Mentors:** Share your thoughts with mentors or colleagues who understand your goals. Their perspective can help you see the bigger picture.

Navigating Career Challenges

Even in a career you love, challenges will arise. Discernment can help you navigate these moments with confidence and intention.

Examples of Common Career Challenges:

- **Handling Difficult Colleagues or Managers:** Use discernment to assess whether the issue can be resolved through communication or if it's a sign of deeper misalignment.
- **Facing Burnout:** Reflect on what's causing the exhaustion and whether it's a temporary challenge or a sign that a change is needed.
- **Deciding When to Leave:** Evaluate whether staying in your current role supports your growth and goals or whether it's time to move on.

Exercise: Career Reflection

Take 10 minutes to reflect on your current role:

1. What aspects of your job bring you the most fulfillment?
2. What aspects drain your energy or feel misaligned with your values?
3. Are there changes you can make to improve alignment, or is it time to consider a new opportunity?

Discernment in Financial Decisions

Aligning Finances with Your Values

Financial decisions are often framed as purely logical, but discernment reveals a deeper truth: money is a tool to support the life you want to create. Making wise financial choices means aligning your spending, saving, and investing habits with your values and long-term goals.

Key Questions for Financial Discernment:

1. **Does this align with my goals?** Does this expense, investment, or financial decision bring you closer to your financial and personal aspirations?
2. **Is this a need or a want?** Evaluate whether a purchase or investment is essential or driven by impulse.
3. **What's the opportunity cost?** Consider what you might have to sacrifice by making this financial choice.

Budgeting with Discernment

Creating and maintaining a budget is a powerful way to ensure your finances reflect your priorities. Here's how to approach budgeting with discernment:

1. **Clarify Your Goals:** Identify your short-term and long-term financial goals (e.g., building an emergency fund, saving for a house, paying off debt).
2. **Track Your Spending:** Review your expenses to understand where your money is going and whether it aligns with your goals.
3. **Prioritize Your Values:** Allocate your budget toward the things that matter most to you. For example, if travel is a priority, adjust other expenses to make room for it.
4. **Avoid Decision Fatigue:** Automate savings and bill payments to reduce

the mental load of managing your finances.

Making Investment Decisions

Investing is an essential part of building long-term financial security, but it requires careful discernment. Here's how to approach investments with clarity:

1. **Educate Yourself:** Learn the basics of investing, including risk tolerance, diversification, and long-term growth. This knowledge will empower you to make informed decisions.
2. **Align Investments with Goals:** Choose investments that match your risk tolerance and financial objectives. For example, if you're saving for retirement, focus on long-term growth strategies.
3. **Seek Professional Advice:** Consider consulting a financial advisor to create a plan tailored to your goals. However, use discernment when selecting advisors to ensure they have your best interests in mind.
4. **Avoid Emotional Decisions:** Market fluctuations can trigger fear or greed. Stay focused on your long-term strategy and avoid making impulsive changes based on short-term trends.

Avoiding Financial Pitfalls

Discernment can help you avoid common financial mistakes, such as:

- **Overspending on Impulse Purchases:** Take a pause before making non-essential purchases. Ask yourself, "Will this bring lasting value or joy?"
- **Carrying Unnecessary Debt:** Evaluate whether borrowing aligns with your goals and ability to repay.
- **Falling for "Get Rich Quick" Schemes:** Use discernment to recognize and avoid investments or opportunities that seem too good to be true.

Integrating Career and Financial Goals

Your career and financial decisions are deeply interconnected. By aligning both with your values and vision, you can create a life that feels purposeful and secure. Here's how to integrate the two:

1. **Define Your Priorities:** Reflect on how your career and financial goals support each other. For example, does your career allow you to save for the future while enjoying your present life?
2. **Set Clear Milestones:** Break your goals into actionable steps, such as earning a promotion, starting a side hustle, or reaching a savings target.
3. **Celebrate Progress:** Acknowledge small wins, such as paying off a debt or securing a new job opportunity, as they build momentum toward your larger goals.

Reflection Exercise: Financial and Career Check-In

1. Write down your top 3 career goals and 3 financial goals.
2. For each goal, reflect on whether your current actions are aligned with achieving it.
3. Identify one adjustment you can make in your career or finances to bring greater alignment.

Closing Reflection: Building a Foundation of Purpose and Stability

Discernment in career and financial decisions empowers you to create a life that feels both meaningful and secure. By aligning your choices with your values and vision, you can navigate challenges with clarity and build a future that reflects your true priorities.

As you continue your journey, remember that career and financial discernment is an ongoing practice. Each decision is an opportunity to learn, grow, and refine your approach. With time and intentionality, you'll find that your career and financial path become a source of fulfillment and empowerment.

10

Discernment in Spiritual and Ethical Choices

Living with Integrity and Purpose

Spirituality and ethics shape the way we view the world and navigate our place within it. These aspects of life connect us to our deepest beliefs, guide our moral compass, and influence how we respond to life's challenges. Whether rooted in a faith tradition, a personal spiritual practice, or a commitment to ethical principles, these choices require discernment to ensure they reflect our core values and lead us to live with integrity and purpose.

This chapter explores how to practice discernment when faced with spiritual and ethical decisions. You'll learn how to align your beliefs and actions, navigate moral dilemmas, and honor your inner truths while respecting the diverse perspectives of others.

The Role of Discernment in Spiritual Choices

Understanding Spiritual Alignment

Spirituality is deeply personal, yet it often intersects with broader cultural, religious, or societal influences. Discernment helps you separate external expectations from your authentic spiritual needs, allowing you to create a practice or belief system that resonates with your values and experiences.

Questions for Spiritual Discernment:

1. **What feels true for me?**
   Reflect on your beliefs and practices. Are they rooted in personal conviction, or are they influenced by external pressures or inherited traditions?
2. **Does this practice bring me closer to peace and meaning?**
   Evaluate whether your spiritual choices foster a sense of connection, purpose, and alignment.
3. **Am I open to growth and change?**
   Spirituality is an evolving journey. Discernment allows you to remain open to new perspectives and experiences while staying grounded in your core truths.

Creating a Personal Spiritual Practice

Whether you follow a specific tradition or take a more individualized approach, creating a personal spiritual practice requires discernment. Here's how to develop one that feels authentic:

1. **Reflect on Your Beliefs:** Spend time exploring what you truly believe about life, purpose, and connection. Write down the principles that resonate most with you.
2. **Experiment with Practices:** Try different spiritual practices, such as meditation, prayer, journaling, or spending time in nature. Notice which ones bring you the most clarity and peace.

3. **Release What Doesn't Serve You:** Let go of practices, rituals, or beliefs that feel misaligned or burdensome.
4. **Revisit and Refine:** As you grow and evolve, revisit your spiritual practice and make adjustments to ensure it continues to reflect your authentic self.

Navigating Spiritual Conflicts

Spiritual conflicts often arise when your beliefs or practices differ from those of others, whether it's within your family, community, or workplace. Discernment helps you navigate these situations with respect and clarity.

Tips for Navigating Spiritual Conflicts:

- **Stay Grounded:** Reflect on your core beliefs and why they matter to you.
- **Practice Empathy:** Try to understand the perspectives and experiences that shape others' beliefs.
- **Set Boundaries:** If someone pressures you to conform to their beliefs, calmly assert your right to make your own choices.
- **Choose Respectful Dialogue:** Approach conversations with curiosity and a willingness to listen, even if you disagree.

Discernment in Ethical Choices

Understanding Ethical Alignment

Ethics are the principles that guide our decisions and actions in the face of moral dilemmas. Practicing ethical discernment means aligning your behavior with your values, even when it's inconvenient or challenging. It's about asking not just, "What's the right thing to do?" but also, "What's the right thing for me to do in this situation?"

Questions for Ethical Discernment:

1. **What are the potential consequences of this action?**
   Consider how your decision will impact yourself, others, and the world around you.
2. **Does this align with my values?**
   Reflect on whether the choice honors your core ethical principles.
3. **What's motivating my decision?**
   Are you acting out of integrity, fear, self-interest, or external pressure?

Navigating Moral Dilemmas

Moral dilemmas often involve conflicting values, priorities, or expectations. Discernment helps you weigh these factors and choose a course of action that aligns with your sense of right and wrong.

Steps for Navigating Moral Dilemmas:

1. **Clarify the Conflict:** Identify the values, principles, or outcomes that are in tension.
2. **Gather Information:** Learn as much as you can about the situation, including potential consequences and perspectives.
3. **Reflect on Your Values:** Revisit your core ethical principles and how they apply to this situation.
4. **Consider the Bigger Picture:** Ask yourself how this decision fits into your long-term vision and the legacy you want to leave.
5. **Seek Wise Counsel:** If you're unsure, consult someone you trust who can offer perspective and guidance.

Living with Integrity

Integrity means living in alignment with your values and ethical principles, even when it's difficult. Practicing integrity requires discernment to navigate situations where external pressures or temptations challenge your convictions.

Tips for Practicing Integrity:

- **Pause Before Acting:** When faced with an ethical decision, take time to reflect and ensure your choice aligns with your values.
- **Be Honest with Yourself:** Acknowledge when fear or self-interest might be influencing your decisions.
- **Accept Imperfection:** No one is perfect, and ethical decision-making can be messy. Learn from your mistakes and strive to do better.

Balancing Inner Truth and External Expectations

The Tension Between Authenticity and Conformity

One of the biggest challenges in spiritual and ethical discernment is balancing your inner truth with the expectations of others. While it's important to honor your own beliefs and values, it's equally important to navigate relationships and societal norms with respect and grace.

Strategies for Balancing Inner Truth and External Expectations:

1. **Know Your Non-Negotiables:** Identify the values and beliefs you're unwilling to compromise.
2. **Practice Compassionate Communication:** Share your perspective with kindness and empathy, even when it differs from others'.
3. **Recognize When to Compromise:** In some situations, compromise may be necessary to maintain harmony or achieve a greater good. Use

discernment to decide when it's appropriate.

The Role of Reflection in Spiritual and Ethical Discernment

Reflection is a powerful tool for spiritual and ethical growth. By regularly reflecting on your choices and experiences, you can deepen your understanding of your values, refine your beliefs, and strengthen your discernment.

Reflection Questions:

- *When was the last time I made a choice that felt deeply aligned with my values?*
- *Have I ever compromised my beliefs out of fear or pressure? What did I learn from that experience?*
- *How do I want my spiritual or ethical principles to guide my life moving forward?*

Reflection Exercise: Crafting Your Ethical and Spiritual Compass

1. Write down your top 3 spiritual beliefs and 3 ethical principles.
2. Reflect on how these guide your daily decisions and actions.
3. Identify one area of your life where you feel misaligned with these beliefs or principles. Consider what changes you can make to bring greater alignment.

Closing Reflection: Choosing Integrity and Connection

Discernment in spiritual and ethical choices allows you to live with integrity, connect deeply with your inner truths, and navigate the world with compassion and purpose. It's not about perfection but about striving to align your actions with your values, even in the face of challenges.

As you continue your journey, remember that spiritual and ethical growth is a lifelong process. By regularly reflecting on your choices, seeking guidance when needed, and staying true to your values, you can cultivate a life of meaning, authenticity, and connection.

11

Discernment in the Age of Digital Distraction

Reclaiming Your Focus in a World That Competes for It

We live in an era where attention has become a currency and nearly everything online is designed to spend it on your behalf. From endless scrolls to constant notifications, from comparison traps to outrage headlines, the digital world pulls at us with both subtle seduction and brute force. And while technology can connect, inspire, and inform, it can also fragment, distract, and overwhelm.

Discernment in the digital age isn't just about managing time. It's about managing energy, emotion, and identity. It's about choosing how, and with whom, you want to engage, rather than passively being pulled by algorithms that don't know your soul.

This chapter is your invitation to approach the digital world with the same clarity, intention, and alignment you bring to your offline life.

The Illusion of Connection, The Reality of Drain

Scrolling can feel like relaxation. A "quick check" of social media can seem harmless. But how often have you found yourself lost in a rabbit hole, comparing your life to a filtered version of someone else's, or feeling mentally cluttered after consuming more than you can process?

The truth is, digital spaces are designed for engagement, not discernment. They are engineered to hold your gaze, stir your emotions, and keep you scrolling, not to make you more present or peaceful.

That's not to say you should leave it all behind. But you should *choose your relationship to it*, rather than letting it choose for you.

Real-Life Vignette: Unfollowing to Reconnect

Carla, a college counselor, realized she was starting every morning with Instagram. Ten minutes turned to thirty, and her mood was often sour before she even made it to the kitchen.

"I didn't even notice it was draining me until I stopped," she said.

She took a break. Just one week. She deleted the app and used that time to journal, stretch, or read a few pages of a book. "By day three," she said, "I felt like I was meeting myself again."

When she returned, she unfollowed any accounts that triggered comparison or consumed attention without adding value. Now, she uses a simple rule: *If it doesn't inspire, inform, or bring joy, it doesn't stay in my feed.*

That's discernment in practice. Not withdrawal, but mindful engagement.

Signs of Digital Misalignment

Here are some cues that your relationship with technology might be out of alignment:

- You feel anxious when you're not online.
- You compare your life unfavorably to others.
- You feel scattered, unfocused, or drained after screen time.
- You default to your phone during silence, boredom, or emotional discomfort.
- You have little time for activities that used to bring joy or reflection.

Practices for Digital Discernment

1. **The Digital Pause**
   Before you click, scroll, or open an app, pause for one breath and ask:

   Why am I opening this?
   What do I hope to feel or achieve?
   Is this a conscious choice or a habit?

   Even just one mindful moment can shift you from autopilot to awareness.

2. **Create "Sacred Tech-Free Zones"**
   Designate spaces or times in your day where your devices don't belong, such as meals, walks, or bedtime through the use of creative rituals. These refuges of digital silence can reconnect you to your senses, your people, and your own inner voice.

3. **Audit Your Attention**
   Once a week, reflect:

   Where did my attention go?
   What content left me inspired or grounded?
   What left me depleted or disoriented?

Let this awareness guide what stays in your digital ecosystem.

4. **Replace, Don't Just Remove**

   It's not enough to limit screen time, you must also fill that space with something nourishing. Stretch. Journal. Call a friend. Take a walk. Stare out the window and do nothing. That emptiness isn't boring—it's where insight begins.

Your Inner Voice Still Exists, But It's Quieter Than the Algorithm

Social media speaks in shouts while your intuition whispers. News feeds are curated for engagement; your inner world is cultivated through stillness. If you want to hear the wisdom within, you have to make space for silence.

That may mean fewer notifications, fewer tabs, fewer voices in your head that don't belong to you. It may mean letting go of the fear of missing out, and replacing it with the joy of *being present*.

Reflection Prompts

- What apps or platforms drain my energy? Which ones replenish it?
- When do I feel most in control of my digital habits? When do I feel most reactive?
- What part of my digital life feels aligned with my values? What part doesn't?
- What boundary would help me feel more spacious and focused this week?

Closing Reflection: Breaking Through the Distraction

In a world that profits from your distraction, discernment is a radical act of self-respect. It says: "I choose where my energy goes. I choose what deserves my attention. I choose what kind of life I want to build."

And that choice, moment by moment, becomes a life of clarity, both online and off.

12

Discernment as a Daily Habit

Living with Everyday Intention

Discernment isn't reserved for major life crossroads; it's a daily practice that shows up in how we spend our time, set priorities, engage with others, and respond to the unexpected. The more we cultivate discernment in our small, everyday choices, the more we shape a life aligned with clarity, purpose, and peace.

The beauty of making discernment a habit is that it frees us from decision fatigue. When our values and intentions guide our daily choices, we don't waste energy second-guessing ourselves. Instead, we act with quiet confidence, knowing our path is consistent with who we are and what matters most.

Tiny Decisions, Big Impact

Think of the dozens, if not hundreds, of choices you make in a day:

- What to eat.
- How to respond to a difficult email.

- Whether to go to the gym or scroll on your phone.
- Whether to speak up or stay silent.

Most of these choices seem small, but together they create the rhythm of your life. When we approach these moments with intentionality, we build a life of discernment one choice at a time.

Real-Life Vignette: The Pause Before the "Yes"

Jasmine, a freelance graphic designer, used to say yes to every client request. She feared turning down work might mean fewer referrals, or worse, losing income. But over time, she realized her schedule was overflowing and her creativity was running dry.

Through coaching, she developed a practice: whenever an offer came in, she would pause for 24 hours before responding. During the pause, she'd ask: "Does this project align with the kind of work I want to do? Does it honor my current energy and boundaries?"

With that habit, Jasmine found herself saying no more often—but the work she said yes to became more fulfilling, better paid, and creatively energizing. Discernment, practiced daily, reshaped her business and her well-being.

Daily Tools for Practicing Discernment

1. **The 3-Minute Morning Preview**
   Start your day with three questions:

   What do I want to feel today?
   What's one choice I can make that aligns with my values?
   What distractions might pull me off course—and how can I gently refocus?

2. **The Midday Reset**

Set a reminder around lunchtime to check in:

Am I reacting or responding today?
Is there a decision I'm avoiding that needs a moment of attention?

3. **The Evening Review**
Before bed, reflect:

Did I live in alignment today?
Where did I override my inner voice?
What am I proud of?

The Role of Ritual in Reinforcement

Habits stick more easily when tied to rituals. Consider pairing your discernment moments with something familiar: a cup of tea, a walk, or journaling. It signals to your mind, this is my moment to reflect.

Closing Reflection: Building the Habit

The practice of discernment isn't confined to mountaintop moments; it's in the morning coffee, the inbox, the traffic jam, and the quiet of the night. As you make daily discernment a habit, you'll find your life aligning more naturally with what you value and envision. Small choices, made wisely, shape a wise life.

13

Navigating Change and Complexity with Discernment

Finding Clarity in the Chaos

Change is inevitable, whether it's a new job, a health scare, a relationship shift, or a global upheaval. In these moments of uncertainty, our first instinct is often to seek control or immediate answers. But discernment invites us to do something else: to slow down, get curious, and make peace with not knowing right away.

Discernment doesn't promise certainty. It offers clarity in the presence of uncertainty, a soft but steady light that helps us take the next step, even if we can't see the whole path.

Real-Life Vignette: When the Plan Changes

Marcus, a high school teacher, had a clear five-year plan: finish his master's degree, become department head, and buy a home near his school. But after a family member fell ill, he found himself unexpectedly relocating across the country to provide care.

"Nothing made sense anymore," he said. "Everything I worked toward felt like it was unraveling." But as he gave himself permission to pause and reflect, Marcus found discernment in questions like:

- *Who am I becoming in this disruption?*
- *How can I serve without losing myself?*
- *What does resilience look like right now?*

Over time, he realized his identity wasn't rooted in titles or timelines—it was rooted in compassion, purpose, and adaptability. He began tutoring online and later launched a blog on caregiving and teaching. The clarity came not through control, but through surrender and reflection.

Discernment Tools for Times of Transition

1. **The "Anchor & Horizon" Practice**
   When things feel unstable, identify:

   Anchor: *What value or truth is still solid, even now?*
   Horizon: *What long-term vision can gently guide you, even if it's blurry?*

2. **Discernment Mapping**
   Draw a circle. Inside, write everything you know (e.g., "I need income," "I'm feeling stuck," "I have support"). Outside the circle, jot what's uncertain. Now focus only on what's inside the circle. Start acting from what's known and trust clarity will expand from there.

3. **The Two-Lens Reflection**
   When facing a complex decision, reflect from two angles:

   Lens of the Present: *What do I need right now to feel safe, supported, and clear?*
   Lens of the Future: *What will my future self thank me for?*

Holding Space for Uncertainty

One of the most courageous acts in discernment is not rushing. We are conditioned to chase immediate resolution, but clarity often requires a season of incubation. Some decisions must marinate before they are ready.
Allow yourself the grace of in-between to say "I'm not ready to decide," to gather input, to listen within. That pause is not weakness; it's wisdom.

Closing Reflection: You Are the Navigator

Navigating change and complexity is never about having all the answers. It's about learning to live and move with intention in uncertain terrain. Discernment gives us the tools not just to survive disruption, but to transform within it. You don't have to know everything; you just need to know what matters now and move from there.

14

Conclusion

The Discerned Life

The Journey You've Taken

If you've reached this final chapter, take a moment to pause—not to rush forward, but to reflect.

You've taken a journey through the landscape of discernment: from its foundations and daily practice to its expression in relationships, career, finances, and spirituality. You've explored your values, listened to your inner voice, and learned how to pause amid pressure. You've questioned assumptions, recognized the influence of others' motives, and deepened your ability to live with awareness.

And that, in itself, is remarkable.

Discernment isn't a single decision or epiphany. It's a way of life—a mindset rooted in intention, clarity, and alignment. It's how we navigate both everyday moments and life-altering crossroads with grace, wisdom, and courage.

Living a Life of Alignment

To live a discerned life doesn't mean you'll never face uncertainty. It doesn't mean every choice will be easy or every outcome will be perfect. Rather, it means you will live in alignment:

- With your values, so your choices reflect who you truly are.
- With your vision, so your life moves toward meaning rather than momentum.
- With your heart and mind, so your inner world is not in conflict but in conversation.

This alignment is your internal compass. And when it's working, you don't have to control everything; you just have to stay close to what's true.

Real-Life Reflection: The Power of a Single Choice

A friend once told to me about how she used discernment in the most ordinary of situations: deciding whether to continue volunteering at a community organization. On the surface, she loved the cause. But week after week, she left feeling depleted, overlooked, and increasingly resentful.

Through reflection, she realized she was volunteering out of obligation and fear of disappointing others—not out of joy or alignment.

One honest conversation, one thoughtful "no," and a simple reallocation of her time—and she found herself energized again. That small act of discernment rippled into her relationships, her work, and her confidence. It reminded her she had the right—and the ability—to choose from a place of truth.

That's the quiet power of discernment. It doesn't always change the world. But it always changes your world.

What to Carry Forward

1. **Discernment is a Practice, Not a Performance**
   You will not always get it right—and you don't have to. Every misstep is part of the refining process. You're not here to be perfect; you're here to be awake.
2. **Your Inner Voice is a Trustworthy Guide**
   In a world filled with noise, trust the still, small voice within. It doesn't shout—but it never lies.
3. **The Pause is a Superpower**
   When in doubt, pause. Breathe. Ask a better question. The answers will come in the space you create.

The Work Is Never Finished—And That's the Beauty of It

Discernment evolves as you evolve. The questions you ask today may not be the ones you'll ask a year from now. And that's not failure—it's growth.

There will be new layers to peel back, new motives to examine, new decisions to face. But now you are equipped. Not because you have all the answers—but because you know how to listen for them.

And when the world pulls you in all directions, when urgency clouds your vision or fear whispers in your ear, you'll know how to come back to yourself.

That is the gift of discernment.

Your Final Invitation

So as this book closes, consider this your beginning. Keep reflecting. Keep listening. Keep choosing with intention.

CONCLUSION

And most importantly,
keep living like your decisions matter, because they do.
Your life is not just the sum of your choices.
It is the story of what you were brave enough to choose on purpose.

Discernment Toolkit

This appendix provides quick-reference tools, exercises, and prompts to support your ongoing discernment practice. Use these pages to refresh your memory, deepen your reflection, or build new habits of intentional choice-making.

1. DAILY DISCERNMENT PRACTICES

Morning Preview (3 Minutes):

- What do I want to feel today?
- What's one choice I can make that aligns with my values?
- What distractions might I need to gently navigate?

Midday Reset:

- Am I reacting or responding?
- Do I need to pause and reflect on a decision?

Evening Reflection:

- Where did I act in alignment today?
- What could I do differently tomorrow?
- What am I proud of?

2. ALIGNMENT CHECK-IN

When faced with a decision, ask:

- Does this align with my core values?
- Does it move me closer to my vision?
- Am I honoring my authentic self or reacting from fear or pressure?
- How will I feel about this decision 10 minutes, 10 months, and 10 years from now?

3. DISCERNMENT IN COMPLEXITY

Anchor & Horizon:

- **Anchor:** What do I know for sure?
- **Horizon:** What am I hoping to build toward?

Discernment Mapping:

- **Inside the circle:** What is known, stable, and actionable?
- **Outside the circle:** What is unknown or uncontrollable?
- Act from the center, not the edges.

Two-Lens Reflection:

- **Lens of the Present:** What do I need right now?
- **Lens of the Future:** What would my future self thank me for?

4. TRUSTING YOUR INNER VOICE

Signs of Intuition:

- Feels calm and clear, not urgent or anxious
- Resonates deeply, even if it lacks full logic
- Aligns with values and long-term vision

Distinguish from Fear:

- Intuition is grounded and quiet
- Fear is loud, rushed, and focused on avoidance

5. QUESTIONS FOR RELATIONAL DISCERNMENT

- Does this relationship reflect mutual respect?
- Is there emotional balance and reciprocity?
- How do I feel before, during, and after our interactions?
- Do I feel safe setting boundaries and are they respected?

6. QUICK PAUSE PRACTICE

When you need to decide quickly, try the STOP Method:

- **S:** Stop
- **T:** Take a breath
- **O:** Observe (what am I feeling, what is influencing me?)
- **P:** Proceed with intention

Keep this toolkit handy as a way to reconnect with the power of intentional choice. Discernment is a skill, and this is your practice space.

Glossary of Key Terms

Alignment:

A state in which your values, actions, and decisions are in harmony with your authentic self and long-term vision.

Anchor:

A known value, belief, or truth that remains stable during times of uncertainty or change.

Daily Discernment:

The habit of applying discernment to small, routine decisions that shape everyday life.

Discernment:

The practice of making wise, intentional choices based on clarity, values, and reflection.

Discernment Mapping:

A visual tool to distinguish between what is known and actionable versus what is uncertain or outside your control.

Intuition:

An inner sense or 'knowing' that guides you, often without logical reasoning. It is calm, grounded, and aligned with your truth.

Lens of the Future:

A perspective that considers the long-term impact of a decision and how it aligns with your future self.

Lens of the Present:

A perspective that evaluates a decision based on current needs, emotions, and resources.

Pause:

A deliberate moment of stillness used to gain clarity before taking action or making a decision.

Reflection:

The process of thoughtfully reviewing experiences or choices to gain insight and awareness.

STOP Method:

A mindfulness-based decision tool: Stop, Take a breath, Observe, Proceed with intention.

Self-Awareness:

The conscious knowledge of your values, motivations, biases, and emotional states.

Values:

Your core beliefs or guiding principles that define what matters most to you in life and decision-making.

Vision:

A clear and inspiring image of the life you want to create, guiding your choices and direction.

Wise Counsel:

Advice from individuals who offer insight, objectivity, and support in alignment with your best interests.

About the Author

I didn't write this book because I had all the answers; I wrote it because, like so many others, I've spent years learning how to ask better questions.

Over the course of my 35+ years in healthcare, first as a Navy-trained hospital corpsman, then as a medical imaging professional, educator, and now a National Board Certified Health & Wellness Coach, I've witnessed just how many decisions shape the trajectory of a life. Some are loud and life-changing. Others are quiet and accumulative. But in every case, the ability to pause, reflect, and choose from a place of alignment makes all the difference.

The Art of Discernment emerged not just from my professional experiences, but from my personal evolution as well. Through service, schooling, missteps, and mentorship, I've come to believe that wisdom isn't about getting it right every time; it's about returning to what matters, over and over again.

I've spent years helping others define their vision of health. This book was my way of helping readers do the same for their inner life by clarifying values, tuning in to their own voice, and making choices with courage and clarity in a noisy, pressured world.

When I'm not coaching clients or creating new health and wellness offerings through my company (Cadre Health), I enjoy traveling, cooking, and learning from the ways other cultures nourish their body and spirit. At heart, I am a teacher and a student who is grateful for every opportunity to make the complex more accessible, and the unseen more understood.

Thank you for taking this journey with me. My hope is that this book doesn't give you answers, but rather helps you listen more deeply to the answers already within.

With appreciation,
   Glen Stancil

You can connect with me on:
🌐 http://www.cadrehealth.org

www.ingramcontent.com/pod-product-compliance
Lightning Source LLC
Chambersburg PA
CBHW061707120626
46550CB00003B/1129